# WINDOWS 10

## Fast and easy start with new operating system of Microsoft. Best tips and tricks!

Table of contents

# Introduction

Now that Windows 10 has been finally released to the market, you need to know how to use it. This book will act as a guide to you on how to perform some of the common tasks with this version of the Windows operating system.

# Chapter 1- Definition

Windows has finally been released to the market. This was on August 1, 2015. The operating system has been developed by Microsoft, which released it for beta testing in September of 2014. As you are probably aware, the users of Microsoft Windows 7 and Windows 8 are getting a free upgrade to Windows 10. However, for you to enjoy the free upgrade, you must be running an eligible version of the Windows 7 or Windows 8 operating system. Users of other versions of Windows OS, must purchase the new version of the OS so as to enjoy using it. When Windows 8 was released, the reception by the market was good. The problems associated with this version of the Windows operating system have now been solved and its users can now laugh. The new version of Windows operating system has brought forward a universal architecture, meaning that developers will be in a position to develop products which can run across the various products of Microsoft. This means that developers will be in a position to develop apps which can run across the various products of Microsoft by use of an almost similar code. The process of making updates to the system has now been made easy, as it will be automatically done on your behalf.

## Chapter 2- How to upgrade from Windows 7 and Windows 8.1 to Windows 10

If you are running any of the above old versions of the Windows operating system, then you can upgrade for free to Windows 10. This can be done by following the steps given below:

Navigate to "Microsoft's Windows 10 download page." You can then click on the link for the 64-bit version of the operating system. However, if your computer has a 32-bit processor, then click on the corresponding link. Note that you do not have to download the operating system, but you can click on the option for "Run."

Download Windows 10

If you need to install or reinstall Windows 10, you can use the tools on this page to create your own installation media using either a USB flash drive or a DVD.

Before you begin

- Make sure you have:
  - An internet connection (internet service provider fees may apply).
  - Sufficient data storage available on a computer, USB or external drive for the download.
  - A blank USB or DVD (and DVD burner) with at least 4 GB of space if you want to create media. We recommend using a blank USB or blank DVD, because any content on it will be deleted.
- Read the System Requirements.
- If you will be installing the operating system for the first time, you will need your Windows product key (xxxxx-xxxxx-xxxxx-xxxxx-xxxxx). For more information about product keys and when they are required, visit the FAQ page.
- For Enterprise editions please visit the Volume Licensing Service Center.

Use the media creation tool to download Windows. This tool provides the best download experience for customers running Windows 7, 8.1 and 10. To learn how to use the tool, go to the Installing Windows 10 using the media creation tool page. Tool includes:
- File formats optimized for download speed.
- Built in media creation options for USBs and DVDs.
- Optional conversion to ISO file format.

Download Tool Now (32-bit version)

Download Tool Now (64-bit version)

You can then be presented with two options, that is, Upgrade now, and create an installation media. Our assumption in this case is that the tool is being run on the PC which needs to be upgraded to Windows 10. If this is the case, just click on "Upgrade this PC now."Note that a clean install of the new version of Windows OS cannot be done as part of the upgrade process. However, the clean install process of this version of Windows will be discussed later in this book.

## What do you want to do?

- ◯ Upgrade this PC now
- ● Create installation media for another PC

What you will see is that Windows 10 will start to be downloaded from the start. You will also notice how fast the Microsoft servers are, since if your Internet connection is okay, the process will take a very short time.

## Downloading Windows 10
Feel free to keep using your PC.

It might be possible that you are just using the current PC so as to create an installation media of the operating system so as to install it on another computer or on multiple computers. If this is the case, then you have to choose the second option, that is, the one for creation of an installation media. The media in this case can be a USB or a DVD. The drive which is to be used can also be chosen and a bootable disc or drive can also be created which can contain both the 32-bit and 64-bit versions of Windows 10.

However, it is good for you to make sure that you have chosen the right edition. This can be confirmed from your PC.

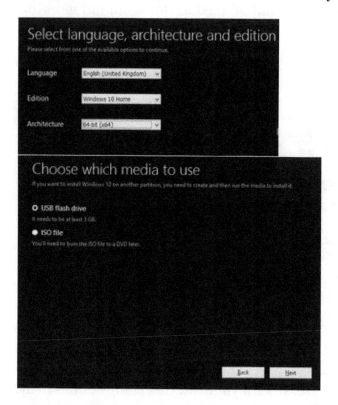

You will then be asked to confirm the license, so make sure that you do that. After this has been done, the installer will perform the task of confirming whether your PC can support the installation of Windows 10 in it. The available space in your PC will also be checked, and then it will also confirm whether updates can be downloaded. An activation key will not be needed for those who are upgrading from Windows 7 or Windows 8 whose versions are eligible.

When you are prompted, just choose install Windows 10 by clicking on that. You will note that the computer will reboot. A Windows logo will also be seen and this will be followed by an option for selecting the language. It is recommended that you select U.S. English as the language.

The installation of Windows 10 into your system will then be done automatically, and all your files and settings will be kept safe. However, if you had installed an antivirus program into your system, then this will not be accomplished. If you read the first part of this book, this is why we said that it is important for you to back up everything that you can't risk losing before beginning the upgrade process.

Once the installation process has completed, you will be taken to the desktop for Windows 10. It is recommended that you give it some time so that it can search for drivers.
Windows 10 will then be ready on your system and then you can begin to work with it. In the next section of this book, we will guide you on how to perform a clean installation of Windows 10 into your system.

## Chapter 3- Clean Installation of Windows 10

When one chooses to upgrade from Windows 7 or Windows 8.1 to Windows 10, then the old files, settings and programs will be dragged to the new version of the Windows operating system. This might not be interesting to some of you. For the users of old versions of Windows other than Windows 7 and Windows 8.1, the upgrade process cannot be supported. This is why it is good for us to discuss how the clean installation process of Windows 10 can be done. However, this process can lead to confusion when it comes to upgrading of the operating system. You can also purchase a new computer which has an installed operating system that you don't want. In this case, you might have to perform a clean installation of Windows 10. Downloading of Windows 10 and creation of an Installation media

Once you have upgraded your system by use of the "Get Windows 10" process, an installation media for Windows 10 must be downloaded before you can install the new version of Windows from scratch.

You should begin by visiting the Microsoft website, and then downloading the Windows 10 media creation tool. With this tool, the correct installation files for Windows 10 will be downloaded and if you need, a USB installation media or installer DVD will also be created. To create an installation media, click on the option labeled "Create an Installation media for another PC."This is shown in the figure given below:

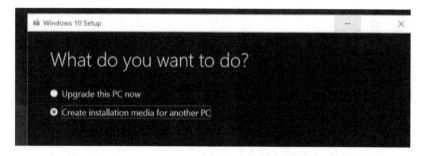

You also have the duty of ensuring that the correct installation of Windows 10 licensed to your PC has been chosen, otherwise, you may experience a problem while trying to do this. The language also needs to be selected and we said that U.S. English is highly recommended. For the case of the version of the operating system, choose either 32 or 64 bit one as appropriate for your system. Most people will want to install the 64 bit version which is still ok. However, it is good for you to make your work easier. This can be done by creating an installation media having both the 32 and 64 bit versions of Windows 10. The installer will then be tasked with the responsibility of choosing and installing the best one, either the 32 or 64 bit version of the Windows 10, and will pick the suitable one.

Select language, architecture, and edition
Please select from one of the available options to continue.

| Language | English (United States) |
| Edition | Windows 10 Pro |
| Architecture | 64-bit (x64) |

Once the installation media has been created, the installation of Windows 10 can be done in the way that you would install any other version of the Windows operating system into your computer.

You should begin by inserting the DVD or the USB drive into your system, and then the system should be restarted. As usual, the boot process should be done from that device that you have inserted. For the users of some Windows such as Windows 8, some BIOS settings might have to be changed by accessing the boot menu.

Once the installer has been launched, just click on "Install Now," and the installation process will be started. A step will be reached in which you will be asked to provide the product key for Windows 10. If you reach this step, just click on the "Skip" button without providing anything, and all will be okay. If you did the free upgrade, then there is no need for you to provide the product key. However, if otherwise, then do the necessary step.

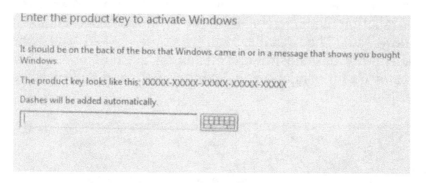

You can then continue with the installation process until you are asked to choose the type of installation that you want. In this case, choose the option for "custom" installation as opposed to the "upgrade" option.

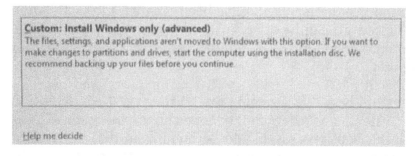

You also have to choose the partition in which Windows 10 should be installed. If you have more than one partition in your system, you can choose to delete all of them, and then choose to install Windows 10 in the space which has not been allocated. In case you have a single partition in which you have installed your current OS, then tell the installer to overwrite it.

Later on, you will be prompted to provide the the product key. Just choose "Do this Later," and continue with the rest of the setup process.

However, once the installation has completed, some people have reported that they have experienced several reboots of the system. If the activation has not occurred even after clearly following the above steps, then there is a command which can be run so as to force this. Just open the command prompt as an administrator by right clicking on the start button and then clicking on the command prompt(Admin). You can also do this by pressing the Window key + X and then selecting the command prompt (Admin). Just type the command given below and then hit the "Return" key:

```
slmgr.vbs /ato
```

If you experience an error after execution of the above command, just restart your system, and then rerun the command again. This might have to be done severally times. If you do not want to do this, you can wait for the OS to be automatically activated. The period taken in this case will depend on how the Microsoft servers are loaded at that time.

## Chapter 4- Setting up a New Local Account in Windows 10

Once the operating system has been successfully installed into the computer, one can choose to create either a Microsoft or a Local account. If you need to make it possible for other users to be able to use your computer, such as Guests and family members, then a new local account has to be set up.

For you to create a new local account in Windows 10, the following steps can be followed:
Launch the "Setting" app, and then click on the option labeled "Accounts."

From the options which are displayed on the left hand side, just identify the option "Family & other users,"and then click on it.

A new window will be displayed and on its right hand side, identify the button "Add someone else on this PC,"and then click on it. This is shown in the figure given below:

In the next window which appears, identify the link "The person I want to add doesn't have an email address,"and then click on it.

You can then click on the "Next" button.

In the next window which appears, identify the link "Add a user without a Microsoft account,"and then click on it. You can then click on the "Next" button, and the next window will be displayed.

In the new window, you will have to specify the username, the password and the password hint for the account. These are shown in the figure given below:

## Create an account for

If you want to use a password, choose somethin
but hard for others to guess.

**Who's going to use this PC?**

> User name

**Make it secure.**

> Enter password

> Re-enter password

> Password hint

Once you are done, just click on the "Finish" button.

Setting up a new Local Account from the Control Panel

Begin by launching the control panel in the small icons view mode.

Click on the option labeled "User Accounts."

You can then click on the link labeled "Manage another account."

In the next window which appears, identify the link "Add a new user in PC settings,"and then click on it. This will just take you to the third step which we carried out in our previous procedure.

## Chapter 5- Switching to a Microsoft Account in Windows 10

While you are logged in to your local account in Windows 10, you might need to switch to your Microsoft account. The reason for this is for one to enjoy some of the benefits that the account offers. Note that as a Windows 10 user, you can choose to create either a local account or a Microsoft account. To perform the switching, kindly follow the steps given below: Launch the "Settings" app. Identify the option for "Accounts," and then click on it.

In the next window which is displayed, move to the left hand side and identify the option labeled"Your account," and then click on it.

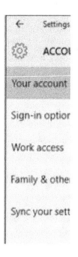

In the next window which opens up, move to the right hand side and identify the option labeled "Sign in with a Microsoft account instead."You can then click on this option.

You will be prompted to provide your email and password. Just provide these and when you are done, just click on the button labeled "sign in."

It might be possible that you do not have a Microsoft account. You might also need to use a new Microsoft account. If this is the case, then identify the link "No Account> Create One!" and then click on it.You will be taken through a series of steps, and a new email for you will be created.

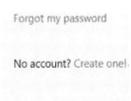

Forgot my password

No account? Create one!.

You will then be prompted to provide the password for your current local account, so just do so. Once you have typed the password, just click on the "Next" button.

## Enter your old password one last time

From here on out, you'll unlock this device using the password or PIN you just set up.

Before we can say goodbye to your local password, you need to provide it one last time.

| Old password |
|---|

(leave blank if none)

Next

The next step is that you will be prompted to create a new PIN other than the password. Once you are presented with the window for doing this, just identify the link "Skip this step," and then click on it.You will then be taken to your Microsoft account.

It might be possible that you need to use the PIN rather than the password. If this is the case, identify the button labeled "Set a PIN," and then click on it. You will be taken through a few steps for setting the PIN and you will be done.

## Chapter 6- Removing the PIN for the Account

It might be possible that you do not need a PIN for the account anymore. You need to note that Windows 10 offers no mechanism for how this can be done. However, there are some steps which we can play around with, and we will achieve this.

To remove the PIN for your account, the following steps can be followed:
Launch the "Settings" app, and then click on the option labeled "Account.".

On the left hand side of the window which appears, identify the option labeled "Sign-in options," and then click on it.

On the window which appears and on the right side of the PIN setting panel, identify the link labeled "I forgot my PIN," and then click on it.

In case the PIN in this case is related to your Microsoft account, then you have to click on the button labeled "Continue" so as to continue.

Are you sure you forgot your PIN?

The only way to set up your PIN again is to reset it. If you use your PIN to access games, social networking, or financial institutions, you'll need to log in from scratch in each of those places after you reset your PIN.

Continue     Cancel

That will act as a confirmation that you want to do away with the PIN.

A confirmation for the password of your account will be needed, and you will be presented with the field to provide this. Just provide the password and then hit the button labeled "Sign in"so as to continue.

You can then provide your alternative email, and a verification code will be sent to you. Once you are done, hit the "Next" button so as to continue.

You can then provide the verification code that you received or that was sent to your alternate email, and this will enable you to reset the PIN. Click on the button labeled "Next" so as to continue.

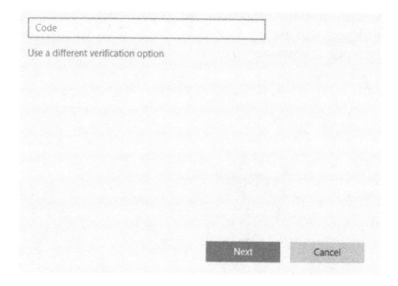

A window for "Set up a PIN" will be presented to you. However, you need not change anything on this window, so just click on the button "Cancel" and the process will be finished.

You can verify whether the process ran successfully by going back to step 2 above. You will notice that the PIN has already been removed.

## Chapter 7- Changing the Password for the Local Account

You might need to change the password for your local account, and most probably for security reasons. In case you forget your password, you can use the password reset drive and this will help you to reset the password. This can be done by following the steps given below:

Just try to log into your account with the wrong password. A message telling you that the password you provided was wrong will be displayed. Just click on the Ok button so as to quit this message.

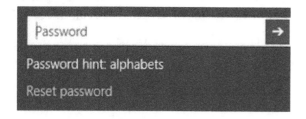

Click on the link labeled "Reset Password," and then insert the password reset drive.

You then have to follow the steps which are necessary in the Password Reset Wizard so as to create a new password.

You can then use the newly created password so as to log into the system.

If you need to quickly change the password, then follow the steps given below:

Press the keys "Ctrl+Alt+Delete" and then click on the link labeled "Change a password."

In the text box for "Old password," type in the current password.

In the text boxes for "New password" and "Confirm password," type in the new password. You can then hit the "Enter" key.
If you need to use the "Setting" option so as to change your password, then follow the steps given below:
Open the "Settings," and then click on the "Accounts" option.

On the left hand side of the window, identify the option labeled "Sign-in options," and then click on it.

Under Password, identify the "Change" button and then click on it.

Provide your current password, and then hit the "Next" button so as to proceed.

In the text field, provide your New Password, and then do the confirmation by retyping it in the "Reenter Password" field.

Type the password hint, and then hit the "Next" button so as to proceed.

## Chapter 8- Setting up a Picture Password in Windows 10

In Windows 10, one can choose to set up a picture password for their account. This feature is most suitable for those who find it difficult to memorize complex passwords for their computers. It ensures that the security of their system is not compromised.

To do this, one has to choose the image which is to be used and then some gestures to be used for setting it up. The good thing about this is that one will not be limited to gestures of the touch screen only, as you can choose to use other devices such as the mouse so as to draw these. To create a picture password for your system, follow the steps given below: Begin by connecting your PC and your Microsoft account together.

You can then open the "Settings" and click on the icon for "Accounts."After that, click on the "Sign-in options."

Identify the button labeled "Add" under the option for "Picture Password," and then click on it.

You will be prompted to provide the password for your Microsoft account, so just do so if prompted. On the left hand side of the window, identify the button for "Choose image," and then click on it. This will allow you to browse for an image which you will choose to use as the picture password. Choose the image of your choice. After the image has been chosen, it is time for you to draw the gesture patterns. These need to be drawn three times and on the same spot on the image, and this will create a gesture pattern for your picture. Once you are done, just save it.

## Chapter 9- Adding a PIN to an Account in Windows 10

You might need to add a PIN to your Windows 10 account if you have not done so. Of course, this is for security purposes. Most people are used to passwords in other versions of Windows. However, Windows 10 supports the use of PINs rather than passwords. The PIN is always in a numerical form, and they make it easy for you to log into your computer, services, and apps by just providing the PIN which is just a simple number.

Most people think that PINs are no secure compared to passwords which are so complex. However, you will notice that PINs are easy to use and especially so on touch-screen devices such as mobile phones and tablets. Once you have created an account on your PC, whether it be the local or the Microsoft account, you will notice that the default feature to be used is the password rather than the PIN.

To add a PIN to your Windows 10 account, just follow the steps given below:

On the left hand side of the window, identify the option "Sign-in options," and then click on it.

On the right side panel and under the "PIN" setting, identify the "Add" button, and then click on it.

Password

Change your ac

Change

PIN

Create a PIN to
easier to sign in

Add

You might be prompted to enter the password for your account. If this is the case, just type the password, and then hit the "Ok" button so as to proceed.

A window for "Set up PIN" will be presented to you. Just provide your PIN, and then do the confirmation by retyping it. Make sure that you choose a minimum of 4 digits for the PIN, as less than 4 digits for a PIN are not supported in Windows 10. This is for the purpose of improving security.

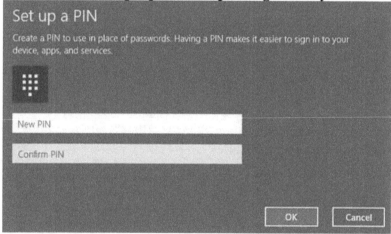

You will then be done. However, in the case of Domain users, you need to note that the PIN is disabled for them.

## Chapter 10- Switching to a Local Account

You might need to switch from your Microsoft account, and then get into your Local account while using Windows 10. Note that we said in Windows 10 one can choose to create either a local or a Microsoft account, depending on what they need.

Suppose that you have been using the Microsoft account, and now you do not need to connect it to your Windows account on your PC. You have to switch to the local account. This can be done by following the steps given below:
Launch the "Settings" app, identify the "Accounts" option and then click on it.

Move to the left side of the window which has been displayed. Identify the option for "Your account," and then click on it.

Move to the right side of the panel, identify the link "Sign in with a Local account instead," and then click on it. This is shown in the figure given below:

Sign in with a local account instead ·


Your picture

Provide the current password for your Microsoft account, and then click on the button labeled "Next" so as to continue.

Current password |

In the next window, you will be asked to provide your username, your password, and then the hint for the password, so just do so. Once you are done, just hit the button labeled "Next" so as to continue.

In the next window which appears, identify the button labeled "Sign out and finish," click on it, and this will switch you from the Microsoft account to your local account.

## Chapter 11- Automatic Sign-in to a User Account

You need to learn how you can be able to control how a user signs in to their account in Windows 10 at start up. The account in this case can be a local or a Microsoft one. In this case, we need the signing in to be done automatically. To do this, kindly follow the steps given below:

On your keyboard, press the "Windows + R" keys. A dialog will pop up, and at its field for type, type "netplwiz," and then click the "Ok" button. This should open the "User Accounts" for you.

You can then select the email address or the User Name of the Local Account or the Microsoft Account that you need the Windows 10 to automatically sign in to once you have booted your machine.

Identify the option "Users must enter a user name and password to use this computer box," and then uncheck it. You can then click on the "Ok" button.

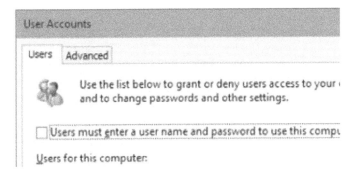

In the next window, you will be prompted to enter the password of the account which you have selected, either the local or the Microsoft account, so just do so. You will be asked to confirm the password, so just do so, and then hit the "Ok" button.

You are then done, and this user will be automatically signed in on startup of the computer. If you need to turn off the automatic sign in for all of the users, then the above option which we have just unchecked, that is "Users must enter a user name and password to use this computer box," must be checked. After you have checked this, just hit the "Ok" button, and the changes will be applied.

## Chapter 12- Microsoft Edge Browser

This browser was introduced for the first time in Windows 10. Most people had been used to the default Internet Explorer which comes installed in Windows. However, Windows 10 broughtwithit a new browser which is Microsoft Edge. The reason why Microsoft introduced this new browser is that it wanted to be able to cope with the changes which have happened to the web since the time of releasing the Windows Explorer browser. Note that Internet Explorer was developed in the year 1995. The figure given below shows what the Edge browser looks like:

The above is how a web page which has been rendered in Microsoft Edge appears to the users. The whole thing looks amazing to the users, hence attracting them.

During the development of this browser, the Microsoft development team was more eying the future. The reason for this is that this browser was built free from the extensibility points of the Internet Explorer which is a legacy browser. Modern security protections regarding the web and the Internet have been implemented in this browser. When you are using this browser and you find it necessary to launch Internet Explorer 11, this can easily be done.

In terms of interoperability improvements, this browser supports over 4,258 of these compared to Internet Explorer. This means that it is not just a contemporary browser, as most of you could think. For users of Windows 10, this browser will be automatically updated when the operating system is being updated. Its management can be done through mobile device management and the Group policy.

The most interesting feature associated with Microsoft Edge browser is that writing on and sharing of web pages can be done with it. Mobile compatibility and edge browsing can also be done in Microsoft Edge. One is also allowed to write and draw on their web pages. If you need to make a web note, you can do this by clicking on the link for this located at the top. This is shown below:

Once you have clicked on that link, you will observe that a secondary menu for doing that will be opened. You will notice that the menu will provide you with the following tools:
Notes
Marker
Pen
Eraser
Clip
These tools will make your work easy, and you will also be in a position to accomplish your tasks.

From the menu for sharing, one can send the image of their choice to OneNote or to their Reading List. This is shown in the figure given below:

The two options are shown in the figure given above, so they can choose to send to any one of them by selecting it. This web browser is interesting in that it will be supported across several devices. This means that the user experience will be greatly improved.

## Chapter 13- How to exclude files from Windows Defender

Windows Defender is an antispyware program which helps to protect computer users from malicious software such as viruses and worms. This program comes built-in in Windows 10 and it is automatically updated together with the operating system itself. The program executes in the background and whenever an action is needed, you are notified of the same. Despite this, one can chose to run a manual scan of their system and it will be okay. However, some people will not want the Windows Defender to scan some of their folders, files, file types, and processes. In this case, these can be excluded. The following are the steps on how this can be done: Launch the app for "Settings,"and then click on the option for "Update & Security."

From the options which are displayed on the left hand side, identify the option "Windows Defender," and then click on it.

On the panel displayed on the right side of the window and underneath "Exclusions," identify the link "Add an exclusion," and then click on it.

It is now time for us to exclude the file. Under the "Files" click on the link labeled "Exclude a file," and then browse for the file in your computer. The file will be excluded.

It might be possible that you need to exclude a folder rather than a file. If this is the case, under the "File locations,"identify the link labeled "Exclude a file location," and then click on it.You can then browse for the folder which needs to be excluded in your system.

You might also need to exclude files of a particular type from the Windows Defender. If this is the case, then under the "File types,"identify the link labeled"Exclude a file extension," and then click on it.You can then provide the extension of the file by typing it in the text box.

It might also be possible that you need to exclude a particular process from Windows Defender. If this is the case, then under "Processes,"click on the link labeled "Exclude a .exe, .com, .scr process," and then browse for the Exclude a .exe, .com, .sc.exe, .com, .scr file in your system.This is shown in the figure given below.

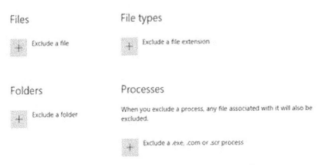

It might be possible that you need to remove an exclusion which you have just added. If this is the case, just click on the exclusion which you have added and then click on the button labeled"Remove."Confirm this by clicking on the button labeled "OK."

## Chapter 14- Addition and Removal of Fingerprint for an Account

In Windows 10, one can choose to either add or remove a fingerprint for their account. Windows 10 brought much improvement in terms of ensuring the security of your system. This is because it now supports biometric authentication in which unique properties such as the retina, facial characteristics, and the fingerprints can be used for the purpose of authentication. This feature is known as the "Windows Hello."The fingerprint can be used for both logging into the system and the securing of purchased apps in the Store. Some of the modern laptops are in support of Fingerprint scanning.

However, in the case of the "Windows Hello" feature in Windows 10, special software and hardware are used for the scanning of the retina and the face. This means that this feature is limited in terms of the number of devices which can support it. For those whose software and hardware cannot meet the requirements of the Windows Hello feature, then once you open the settings of your computer, you will not find this feature.

To add or remove the fingerprints from your account, follow the steps given below:

Launch the app for "Settings," and then click on the option labeled "Accounts.".

On the left hand side of the window which appears, click on the option labeled "Sign-in options."

On the panel which appears, move to the right side and identify the button labeled "Set up."This can be found underneath the "Fingerprint."

You can then click on the button labeled "Get started" so as to proceed.

Perform the verification by providing your PIN.

Follow the onscreen instructions so as to scan your finger. The scanning of the finger will be done multiple times and at various angles, so that the impression of it is saved.

When done, click on the button labeled "Close" so as to finish the setup. If you wish to add another scan of a fingerprint, click on the button labeled "Add another,"and you will be in a position to do that.

If you need to remove a particular fingerprint, then underneath the "Fingerprint" and in "Sign-in options,"identify the "Close" button, and then click on it.

## Chapter 15- Adding a Display Language

With Windows 10, one can change the display language from English to any of the 140 other available display languages. After installation of Windows 10, you will realize that you are only allowed to choose from a single language. However, if you need, many languages can be added, and you will be in a position to switch between them.

For you to add a display language in Windows 10, follow the steps given below:

Launch the app for "Settings" and then click on the option labeled "Time & language."

Move to the options which are displayed on the left panel, and click on "Region & language."

On the panel displayed to the right and under "Languages,"identify the option labeled "Add a language," and then click on it.

You can then browse to the language which is to be added. Once you find it, click on its name.

The language that has been clicked should appear as an additional language in the option for "Region & language."

The language pack also needs to be installed. You can then click on the language which has been added and then click on the "Options."

The language pack can then be downloaded by clicking on the "Download" button.

Now you are aware of how a new display language can be added to Windows 10. However, once you have added this, you might need to change it. Remember that we said that there about 140 languages which are supported in Windows 10. One can switch between these languages. However, before doing this, one has to add the language pack to their system.

To change a display language in Windows 10, follow the steps given below:
Begin by launching the app for "Settings," and then click on the option labeled "Time & language."

Some options will be displayed on the left hand side of the window. Identify the option "Region & language," and then click on it.

Under "Languages," which can be found on the right side of the panel, identify the name of the language to which you want to change the display language, and then click on it.

Once you have clicked on the language name, find the button labeled "Set as default" underneath the name of the language, and then click on it.

After that, the language will have been changed successfully. However, for the changes to be applied, you have to sign out and then sign back in. If you do not do this, you will continue using the old language you were using.

Press the keys "Alt + F4" and then choose the option for "Sign out."

After the sign out, sign in once again. You will notice that your display language has been changed.

# Chapter 16- Changing the Language of the Keyboard

Windows 10 gives its users the option of choosing the language for their keyboard from the 140 available languages. You can also add languages to the keyboard. Once the languages have been added, one can switch between them as they type in an application such as Word 2016. Note that the language pack must be added to your system before one can add this language as the one for their keyboard. This chapter will guide you on how to change the language for your keyboard in Windows 10.

This can be done by following the steps given below:

Launch an application which requires an input to be entered via the keyboard. This can be any app, and a good example of this is Word.

On the task bar, move to its extreme right side, identify the icon "ENG," and then click on it. If you are using another display language, then click the appropriate icon.

You can then click on the language which needs to be used. You will then realize that the "ENG" icon will change to the default one for the language you have chosen.

On your opened Word, just try to type and you will realize that you will type in the language which you have changed to.

If you need to change back to English or any other language which you like, just follow the steps which we have discussed above and all will be well.

Sometimes, one might need to use a keyboard shortcut so as to change the language of their keyboard. This can be done by following the steps given below:

Launch an application which requires input to be provided via the keyboard. A good example of this is Word.

Press the keys "Window + Spacebar."

You can then cycle between the various languages by pressing the spacebar key. Once you find the language that you need, just click on it.

Try to type on the application which you have opened, and you will notice that the language will have been changed to what you need.

## Chapter 17- Changing the Language of Cortana

Currently, the Cortana app is in support of seven languages. These languages include the following:
American English
British English
German
Italian
Spanish
French
Mandarin Chinese
Note that the default language for Cortana is American English. However, one can change this to any of the above languages. Once you have changed this, Cortana will start to speak in this language and also offer content which is in this new language.

The language for Cortana can be changed by following the steps given below:
Begin by installing the new language which you need Cortana to start speaking in.

The installation of the language pack will be finally completed. Under the "Languages," identify the option labeled "Set asdefault," and then click on it.

| Set as default | Options | Remove |
| --- | --- | --- |

On the left side of the panel, identify the option "Speech," and then click on it.

Under the option written "Choose the language you speak with your device," choose the language which you just installed.

For the case of non-native speakers of the newly installed language, identify the option which is next to "Recognize non-native accents for this language," and then check it.

# Chapter 18- Setting the Frequency of Feedback

In Windows 10, there is the feedback app which gets the feedback from the users of the system in real time. An example of this is once an installation of a new display language has been done. What happens is that this app will ask you about how easy you found it to install the language. The scale for this can range between 1 to 5. The feedback is sent back to the Microsoft development team so that they can do something if problems occur.

It is possible for one to control how feedback is requested from them by this app as you use the operating system. By default, the frequency for this is set to automatic. However, one can change it to once in a day, a week, a month, or even never. Other than the feedback, information about the usage and data will also be collected so that the Microsoft team can improve their services and products.

For you to edit the feedback frequency, follow the steps given below:
Begin by launching the app for "Settings,"and then click on the option labeled "Privacy."

From the right side of the window, identify the option "Feedback & diagnostics," and then click on it.

It is now time for us to change the frequency of the feedback. Move to the right side of the panel and under the option labeled "Windows should ask for my feedback," you will find a dropdown list. You can choose the frequency from this list.

You might also need to change the setting for usage data. To do this, move to the right side of the panel and under the option for "Send your device data to Microsoft,"select from the drop down list which is given there.

## Diagnostic and usage data

Send your device data to Microsoft

Full (Recommended)

This will then be set to what you have selected, and all will be okay.

# Chapter 19- Adding a Family member to the Device

Multiple accounts for each different usercan be created in Windows 10. The users of each of the accounts will be in a position to personalize their own accounts to what they need. With users, one can control how and who can make certain changes to the computer and the users who are allowed to access certain features.

With Windows 10, the members of your family can be added under Microsoft family. It is after this that these members will be able to sign into their accounts after they have signed into their Microsoft accounts. In this family, there are adult and child accounts, in which the adult accounts are capable of controlling the child accounts. This means that they can determine what the child accounts can have.

To add a family member in Windows 10, follow the steps given below:
Begin by launching the app for "Settings," and then click on the option labeled "Accounts."

From the options which are displayed on the left hand side of the window, click on the "Family & other users" option.

On the right side of the panel and under "Your Family,"click on the link labeled "Add a family member."

## Your family

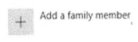

Add your family so everybody
desktop. You can help kids sta
time limits, apps, and games.

Add a family member

Learn more

## Other users

You might be prompted to enter the PIN or the password for your account. If this is the case, just provide that and then click on the "sign in" button.

Identify the radio button which is next to "Add a Child" or "Add an Adult," and then check it.

You can then provide the email address of the family member who is to be added, and then click on the "Next" button so as to continue.

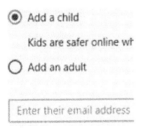

⦿ Add a child

Kids are safer online wh

◯ Add an adult

Enter their email address

Click on the "Confirm" button so that you can be continued.

Once you have done that, an email will be sent to the email of the family member from Microsoft which will act as an invitation for them to become part of your Microsoft family.

Microsoft

.... would like you to join their family as an adult. If you accept, you'll be able to approve requests, change kids' settings and get weekly activity reports.

Accept Invitation

This invitation will expire in 14 days.

The family should then follow the instructions which are given in the email and they will join the Microsoft family. After this, you will observe the account listed in "Your Family" in the Settings.

# Conclusion

Windows 10 has finally been released to the market. For those who have been waiting for it, you can now enjoy using it. There have been   numerous changes in the history of Windows operating system. For the users of Windows 7 and Windows 8.1, you can enjoy a free upgrade from these to Windows 10. However, for this to happen, you must be running a legitimate version of these operating systems, otherwise, you will not be qualified for the free upgrade. Note that once you have upgraded from Windows 7 or Windows 8.1 to Windows 10, all of the settings and files which were contained in the old system will be copied into the new system. This might not be interesting to some of you. This is why some people opt for the clean installation of Windows since all of the old files will be moved to the "windows.old" folder. These can then be deleted later.

The process of preparing for the clean installation of Windows 10 has been discussed in this book, so you should now understand  how this can be done. While one is logged into either the local or the Microsoft account, they can perform a switch to the other account. For security purposes, Windows 10 has introduced the use of PINs rather than a password. This allows the users to easily remember their PIN rather than a complex password. The PIN should have a minimum of 4 digits. One can also choose to use the picture password for authentication, in which one will be required to draw gesture patterns. This is an interesting feature for authentication purposes in Windows 10.

Biometric authentications by use of fingerprints, facial characteristics, and retina are supported in Windows 10. The Windows Defender, which is an antispyware program, also comes built-in to Windows 10. It runs in the background and is updated together with operating system. Whenever an action regarding security is needed, it notifies you.

www.ingramcontent.com/pod-product-compliance
Lightning Source LLC
LaVergne TN
LVHW052315060326
832902LV00021B/3912